Watercolor
Value to Color Parallel

SEE the Value and Match the Color

Barbara A Parish

Writer and Illustrator

Barbara's Note

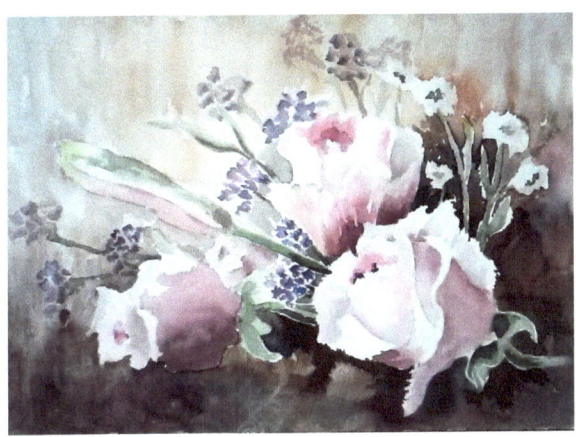

Working with Values is exciting yet intimidating!

Each color has many values.

> **Intense = Dark,** straight from the color tube, slight water added.
> **Neutral = Medium,** a small amount of water mixed with color.
> **Tone = Light,** lots of water mixed with color.

Working with Light, Medium, and Dark Values will create the illusion of 3-dimensional objects on a flat piece of paper.

Example:
* A tree will look like it's standing tall reaching to the sky.
* The image of a ball sitting on paper looking like it's ready to roll.
* Follow a path into the distance.

Working with Light, Medium, and Dark values will tell your visual story.

Painting with watercolor has many facets to learn. Enjoy each learning step along the way.
THINK BEFORE YOU PAINT!

This is a BIG part of becoming a Watercolor Artist.
Design the page
Work out the Values
Create the Texture
Choose Brush Technique

YOUR JOB starts with holding the brush loosely. Watercolor is a GENTLE medium.
- Let the brush create the shape using a gentle stroke.
- Each brush is made to perform a specific stroke.
- Bring a color to the mixing area on the palette. Then bring the color to the paper.
Mastery
Read ~ Understand ~ Apply

MY JOB to share my painting experience with you.
- Matching a Color to its Value
- Working with the Color Wheel
- Color Intensity and Tone
- Color Temperature Warm or Cool
- Color Schemes
- Color with Textures

I will give you the encouragement to manage Value to

Color using painted examples and instruction, will enable you to express yourself with the Watercolor Medium. Practice the examples to grow as an artist!

Dedication

I dedicate this book to watercolor painters trying to figure out this amazing world of color.

Let's enjoy the adventure together!

Copyright

Table of Contents

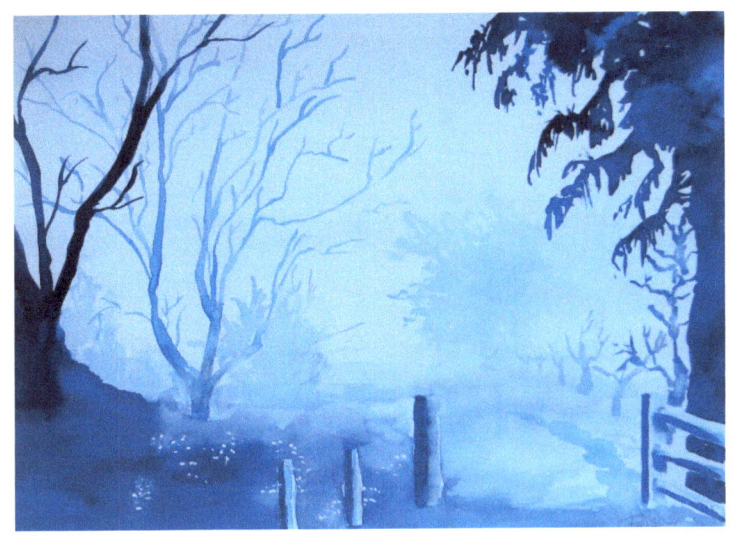

1

Working With Value

What is value?

The above painting example is a Value Study.
Viewing the example, do you feel the visual draw into
the painting? The entrance fence brings your eye into
the painting and values visually lead your eye up the
path into the distance? You are sensing the
3-dimensional pull of value, line, shape, size, and
placement.

Now, let's take it one step further.
Using Light, Medium, and Dark values will give
objects form and draw your eye into the distance.
Notice the three values Light, Medium, and Dark that

make the fence posts look round or square. Be aware of the landscape fading into the distance.

Learning to use values is a must-do!

Use a Sketchbook For Value References

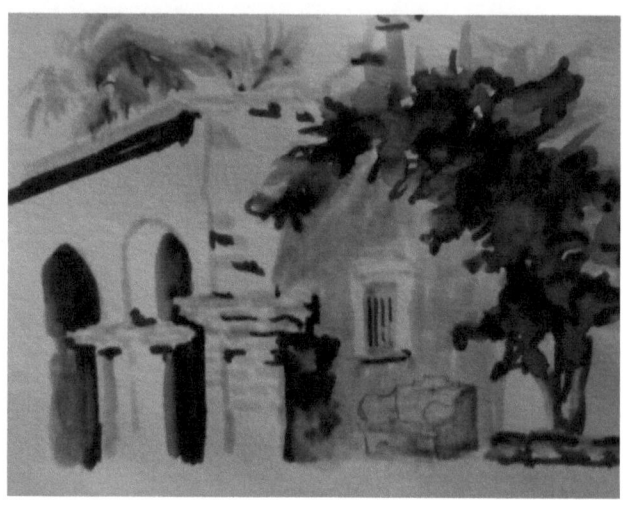

One of my favorite places to sketch is Mission San Juan Capistrano. I SEE a possible painting everywhere I look. Above find a value sketch of one small area of the mission. In this sketch, I use water-soluble pens to release edges and change values with a damp brush.

This thumbnail line and detail sketch of the mission bench I will use as a reference for my painting.

A sketch will grab the essence, line, and detail of the

subject.

Know the subject before you try to paint it.

The Sketchbook is The Key

Gathering all your information before you wet your

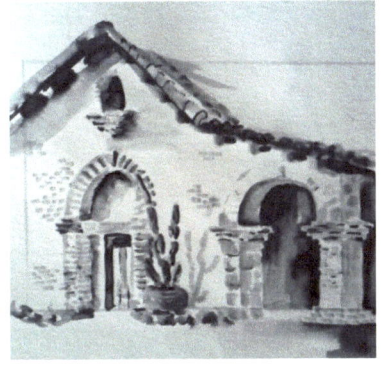

brush is a smart move. This sketch layered with information helps me design my painting by observing line, shape, value, and placement.

I chose church steeples and stained glass to create a

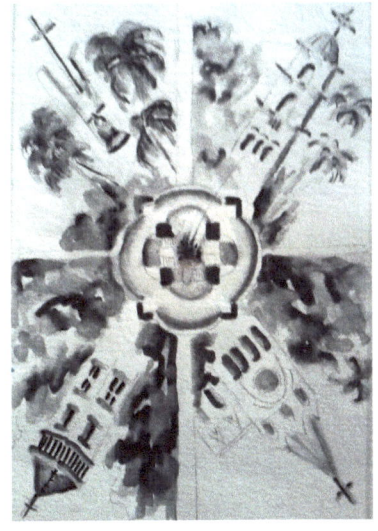

visual story. Using values are what make form and give interest to this composition. In the future, I can use this reference idea to start another painting.

Keep your ideas, sketches, and color schemes in a sketchbook for easy reference.

Painting on Location

A big part of sketching and painting on location is how

to handle the viewers interested in what you are doing. If you are self-conscious painting in front of an audience, stand up, acknowledge the viewers, and talk with them as they observe your painting. If you feel comfortable painting while being observed, continue painting. This is good practice for you to talk and paint at the same time. People love this, and might buy the painting you are working on. Realize that they are in awe of you and what you are doing.

What's Happening in My Art World

I remember painting at the Mission San Juan Capistrano one afternoon. I was focused, making decisions on brush strokes and color value when I heard someone cough. I turned with a surprised look on my face to see 20 people watching me paint. As I stood up, they started clapping and talking with me. We observed the painting together, and I answered questions. What a fun experience.

Thumbnail Sketch

Using a sketchbook will help make decisions on designing the page, working out a color scheme, and choosing a format.

Using a 3"x4" size thumbnail sketch helps make decisions on format, values, center of interest, and color scheme.

Format ~ Vertical or Horizontal
Values ~ Light, Medium, and Dark
Center of Interest ~ Subject of Visual Story

Background, Middle Ground, and Foreground
Designing the space on a flat piece of watercolor paper can be intimidating. Divide the space into three unequal areas.

Create Distance Using Value

The **Background** will be the light/cool value.

The **Middle Ground** will be the neutral/middle value.

The **Foreground** will be the intense/warm value.

The top edge of the paper called the **Background**. The middle of the paper called the **Middle Ground** The bottom edge of the paper called **Foreground**.

As you build your painting skill, you can change the values of Background, Middle Ground, and Foreground by switching color value around.

Important: Color temperature will always stay cool in the background, neutral in the middle, and warm in

13

the foreground.

The Parts of Foreground, Middle Ground, and Background Must be Unequal in Size

High Horizon Line   **Low Horizon Line**

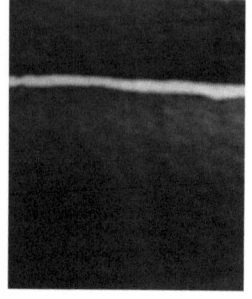   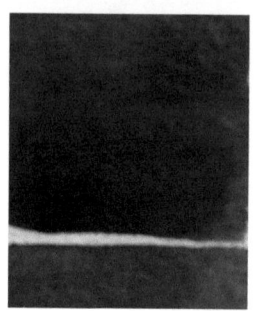

While designing your composition, think ahead, always decide where to put the Horizon Line before you start to paint. You have two choices as shown above.

High Horizon ~ The high horizon line gives a larger area for foreground and middle ground.
Low Horizon ~ The low horizon line gives a larger area for middle ground and background.

Guide to Value
To start using values, keep it simple. I just explained how using three values, Light, Medium, and Dark, would make form. Now, let's add two more values to make a complete Five Value Scale.

Five Value Scale

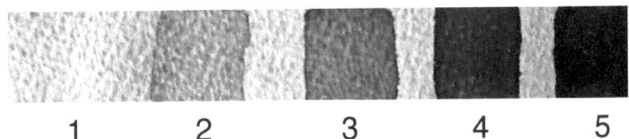

1	2	3	4	5

I suggest you paint this Value Scale for your reference. Place were you can see it while painting. This will keep you on track with values. Watercolor painters start their painting with light values.

Draw five squares on watercolor paper, just like the example above. Start with intense color right out of the tube a value #5. With a damp brush, pick up the dark color and place a half dollar size puddle in the palette mixing area. Take dark color from palette mixing area and paint in the #5 square. Then, add water to the dark color to lighten, and fill in #4 square. Do this process with #3 and #2, lightening the value until the value in #1 square equals the light value of watercolor paper.

Painting a Value Scale will teach you how to create the correct value and how the value scale works when introducing color. Repaint the value scale until you have it perfect. Painting the correct values may not be easy, do as many times as necessary. The more you paint a value scale the more you learn about values. Enjoy the process and work at it.

Worth The Effort to Learn

Five Value Scale

Light

Medium Light

Middle Value

Medium Dark

Dark

Watercolor Painting Process

* Use the light values to lay in your first wash. The light value can be "free form" painting outside the line, and leaving areas of white paper.

* Use the middle values to paint the second wash. Modeling shapes and painting the space behind the shapes.

* Be selective using the dark values, work around the Center of Interest area creating dark and light contrast. The contrast will draw the viewer's eye to the Center of Interest.

* Direct the viewer's eye to the Center of Interest area using various contrasts like warm against cool, light against dark and hard edges against soft edges.

The Five Value scale is easier to use if you are a new painter. Feel comfortable painting with the Five Value Scale before challenging yourself to use the Ten Value Scale.

Ten Value Scale
Looking out at the landscape, you will SEE more than ten values. Let's keep it simple and create with a Ten Value Scale.

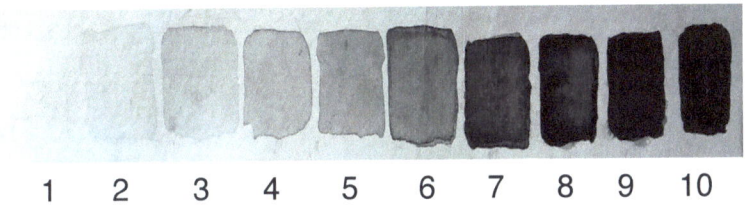

1   2   3   4   5   6   7   8   9   10

The excitement of working with color stretches your imagination and creates a composition that has visual excitement.

Use the same principles as the Five Value Scale. The Ten Value Scale can make your painting more interesting by adding more values. The Middle Value is #5.

Working With Ten Values is a Joy

Squint your eyes, and notice the change of value in each of the ten squares. Each value square connects with a color. Practice painting the value scale, have some fun, use different shapes.

With watercolor, the value scale starts with a #1 for the light value. The reason for this is watercolor painters lay in a light color wash first, then build up to the darks.

The next step in working with values is to match a color to each value. Chapter 2 will help you understand the Color Wheel.

Train your eye to **"SEE Value as Color."**

Notes and Ideas

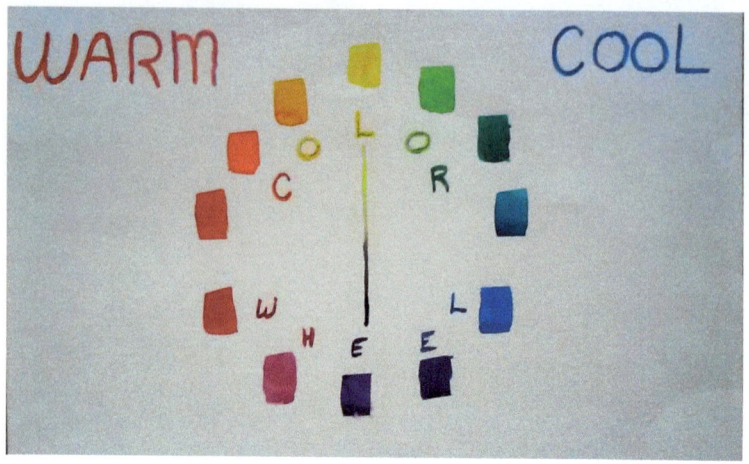

2

Working With Color

Value to Color
Water is The Key to Color Values
Color Wheel
Warm/Cool Temperature
Mixing Gray Values
Mixing Dark Values

What is Color?
Color electrifies your composition. Color, value, and color temperature are in the landscape we see every day.

One suggestion I have to help a painter to recognize Color, Value and Temperature, sit outside on your patio or along a rushing stream. Close your eyes, listen to the sounds of nature, and ponder for a while calming your spirit. Now open your eyes look at what is in front of you.

* Do you SEE the variety of warm and cool color temperature?
* Do you SEE the light, medium, and dark color values on objects and in the landscape?
* Be aware of the placement of objects, one in front of another or behind another.
* The value of quiet cool color push objects into the distance.

Remember, it takes a minimum of three-color values to make a form. Look for a color value change in each shape and in the landscape.

While painting, if you feel the color needs to change, change it! Keep the same value and change the color. Make sure the color temperature remains the same.

Cool Color Values   Warm Color Values

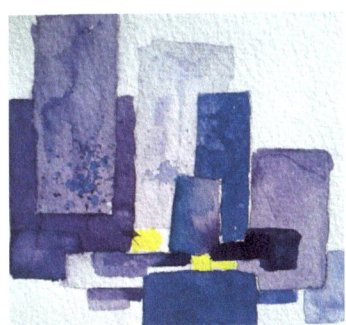
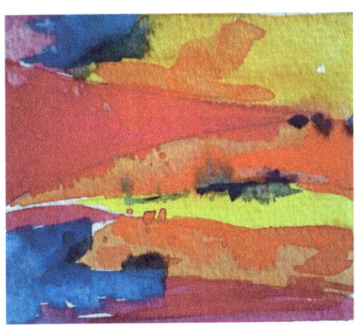

Primary Colors Red, Yellow, and Blue

The Color Wheel is a valuable Color reference tool. Across from each color, find the complement color. Add a small amount of complement color to the primary color, changing the two colors to gray.

Paint examples of all the Color Schemes listed below. Working with a Primary Color plus its Complement Color will add unity to your painting.

Example:

Directly across from the color Red, on the Color Wheel, fine the complement color Green. A touch of green can gray the red color. Grayed colors are for the Middle Ground and shadows. The trick for mixing grayed colors is the amount of complement color mixed with the Primary color. Red and Green, use equal amounts to mix a true gray color. Less Green in the Red will mix a reddish gray color. Less Red in the Green will mix a greenish gray color.
Got it?

The difference between grayed color and a muddy color is the clarity and transparency of the grayed color. If you use a cool temperature primary color scheme, NO MUD will happen. The same with a warm temperature primary color scheme, NO MUD will happen. The trouble starts with mixing a warm red color with a cool green color, creating a dull flat mud color. Mud color has lost luminosity and transparency.

22

Working with Warm Complement Colors
Red/Green

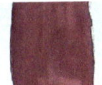

Always work toward clarity and luminosity.

Working with Warm Complement Colors
Yellow/Purple

Mingling the primary color with its complement will create grayed and neutral colors.

Working with Warm Complement Colors
Blue/Orange

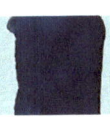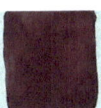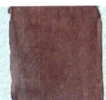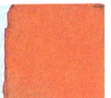

Using the Primary Color with its Complement will keep the transparent color luminous and vibrant.

Plan your painting before you pick up a brush.

Color Wheel
The Color Wheel is set up to easily locate color combinations and recognize cool color and warm color.

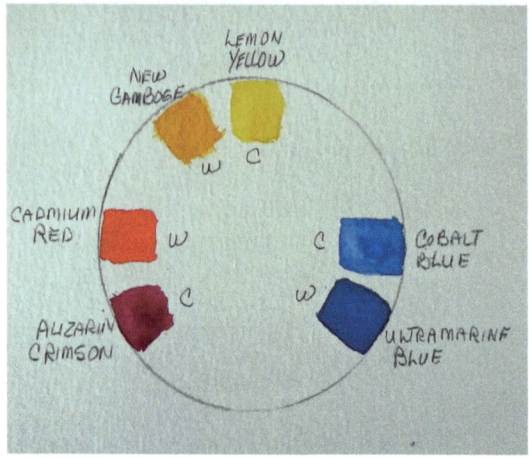

Each cool color primary has a warm color primary. These cool and warm primaries are placed next to each other in your palette.

Cool Temperature

Lemon Yellow   Alizarin Crimson   Cobalt Blue

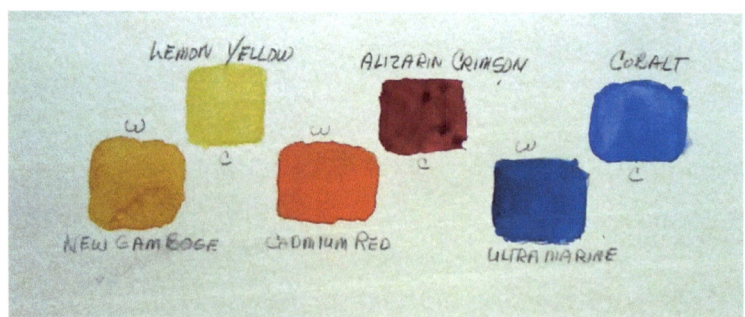

Warm Temperature

New Gamboge   Cadmium Red   Ultramarine Blue

Primary Colors:

Red, Yellow and Blue are the primary colors on your color wheel. Mixing other colors cannot create these colors.

**Yellow, Red, and Blue
stand alone as original color**

  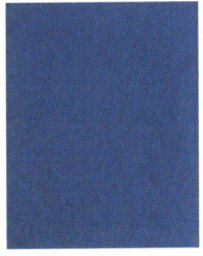

The fun starts when you mix one primary color with another to get a secondary color.

Secondary Colors:
Red mixed with Yellow will create an Orange.
Blue mixed with Red will create a Purple.
Yellow mixed with Blue will create a Green.

  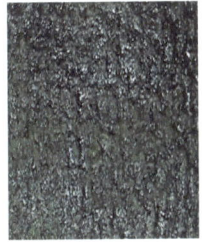

I think it is fascinating to work with the color wheel. Take time to understand what I am presenting to you. Remember the best way to learn something new is to understand the principle, and then apply.

Tertiary Colors:

Mixing a primary color with secondary color will give a Tertiary Color.

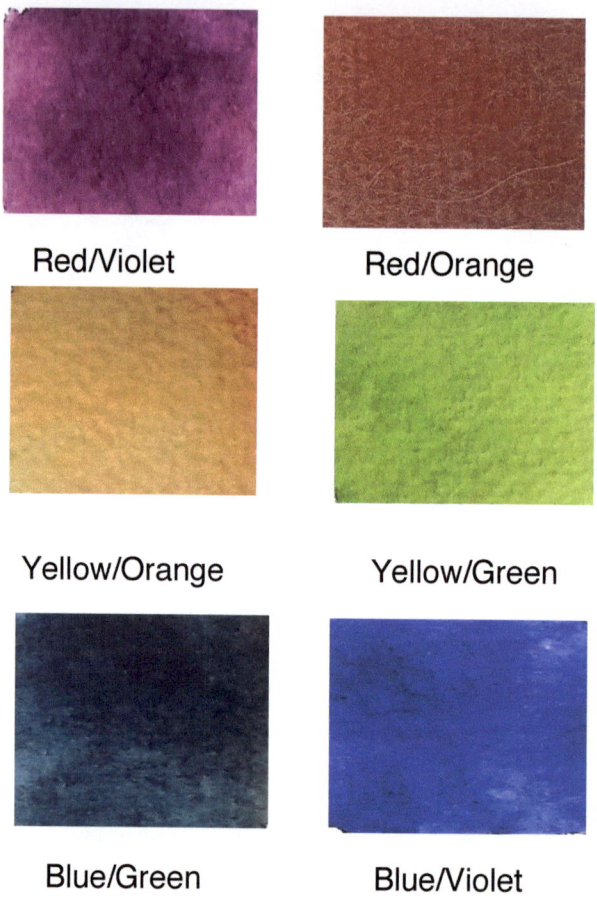

Red/Violet	Red/Orange
Yellow/Orange	Yellow/Green
Blue/Green	Blue/Violet

The doing is what will clarify the action.

Watercolor looks fresh at the first stroke of color. Let it alone. Guard against wipeouts, scrubbing the paper, and changing your mind on design or color temperature half way through the painting. All this will give an overworked look.

Warm/Cool

My class color chart helps you see Warm Colors on the left side and Cool Colors on the right side. Across from a warm color, find its complement color.

Hue ~ true color or shade

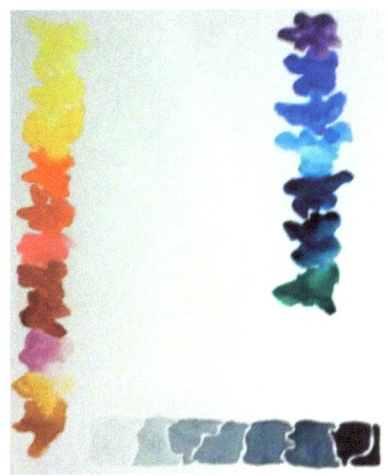

The complement of Yellow is Purple.
The complement of Orange is Blue.
The complement of Red is Green.

I find it easier to teach color theory using a line of warm colors and a line of cool colors. At the bottom, I placed a value scale. Take the time to paint this color chart to use as your reference while you paint. On the other hand, if you prefer, paint the color wheel separate from the value scale for your reference.

Value

Every intense color, meaning color straight out of the tube, will change the value by adding water. Using this color chart, can you see how color matches to value? Put the value scale up to a color on your mixing palette or painting. SEE what color matches the light side or the dark side of the value scale.

Watercolor paint dries lighter on the paper than the

27

value you see when mixing on the palette. Use less water to keep the intense color a shade or two darker than the color you want to use.

Palette

I keep colors in the same order in the palette. That way I know exactly where the color is when I reach for it. Each Primary color, Yellow, Red, and Blue, has a warm and cool color placed next to each other on the palette. Mix warm color with warm color, and cool color with cool color. Do not mix temperature. We will talk about temperature in Chapter 4.

What is MUD?

Have you heard about MUDDY color? Mud color has no luminosity or transparency. A flat, dull color hides the white paper from showing its beauty through the color. The magic of transparent watercolor on paper depends on the clarity of color and the transparency that allows the white paper to illuminate thru color.

Mixing Dark Value

Yellow, Red, and Blue are the primary colors. When mixed in equal amounts, the color turns blackish.

Yellow, Red, and Blue, takes on a Brownish Black color by adding more Yellow. Yellow, Red, and Blue take on a Bluish Black color by adding more Blue.

Remember to keep the color temperature in mind when mixing colors.

Cool Color with Cool Color
Warm Color with Warm Color

Using transparent Red, Yellow, or Blue to make your dark colors will add excitement and illuminate the white of the watercolor paper.

Notes and Ideas

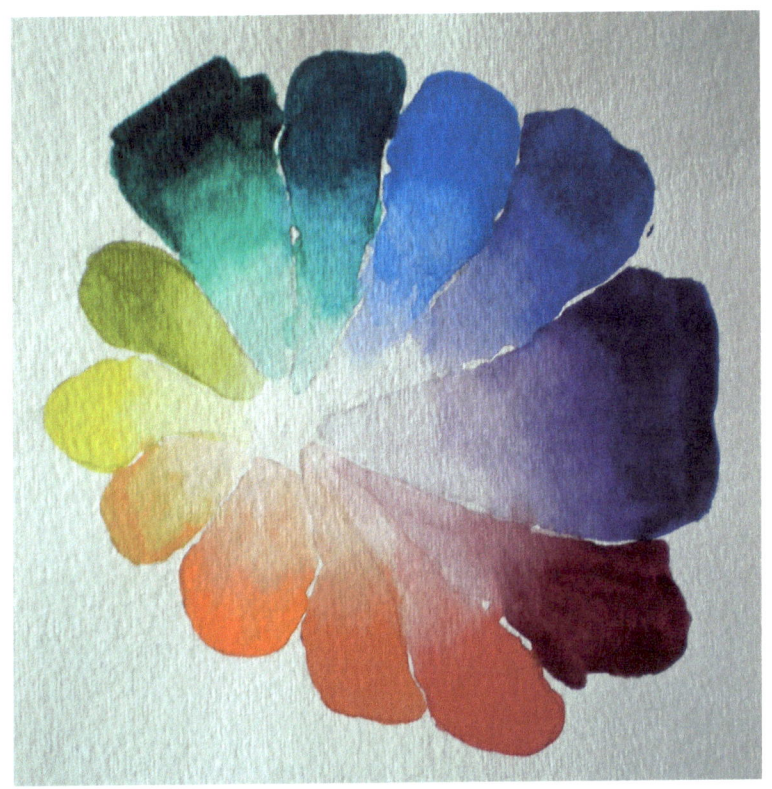

3

Intensity, Tone, and Temperature

Color Intensity
Color right out of the tube

Color Tone
Color lightened with water

Color Temperature
Warm or Cool

The example below shows the illusion of a box sitting on a table. See two insides and two outsides of this box. The inside is lit by the light source above and shows a lighter value. The outside of the box is facing away from the light source, showing a darker value. Each box side has a different value because of the light source hitting the various angles of the box.

Shadow   Sun Light

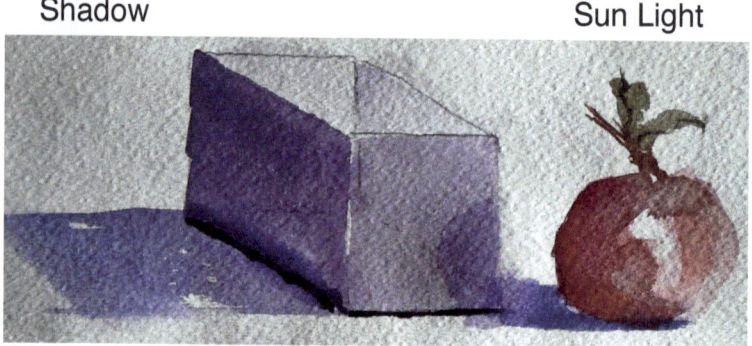

The apple shows a light, medium, and dark color to give the illusion of being round and sitting on the table. The apple is blocking the sunlight causing a shadow on the box.

Light, Medium, and Dark
Tone, Neutral, and Intense

Each Color Has a Different Range of Values
The warmer lighter colors like Yellow, Orange, and Red have fewer value changes. The darker colors like Purple, Blue, and Green have a full range of values from light to dark.
A change of color value creates form and distance.
To paint values, here is the formula.

The **lighter** value: more water, less color
The **darker** value: less water, more color
Intensity = Color from Tube
Tone = Color from Tube, add water

Change Value by Adding Water

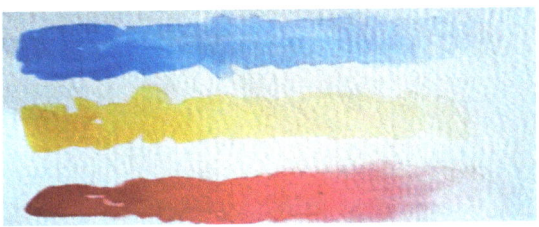

Intense   **Tone**

Water is the key to changing values when working
with watercolor. The more water used with color, the
lighter the color.

Value Range

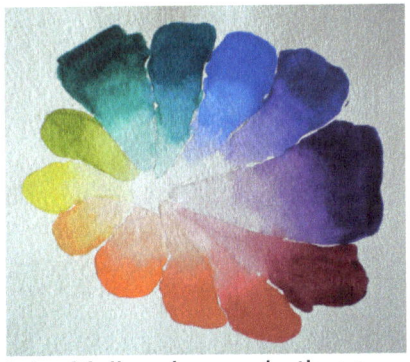

The intense color
appears on the outside
of the Flower Petal.
SEE the intense color
changing to a tone by
adding water.

Look at the size of the petals. Yellow has only three
values of light color, with short petals. While the
Purple petal is longer and wider than the rest, its
values will take the full 10 Value Scale.
Understanding the many values each color can

produce will add excitement to the visual story, creating an eye-catching painting.

On the lighter side of the Flower Petal, find warmer colors: Yellow, Orange, Red. These warm colors have less pigment and will make fewer values of color.

The darker side of the Flower Petal, find cooler colors: Purple, Blue, and Green. These colors have more pigment and produce more values.

View the petals, and notice the length of each color petal. The range of values changes with the petal size. A good practice is to make your own Flower Petal reference and keep it alongside your easel. Painting with values is the key to the illusion of form and distance on the page.

Cool and Warm Color Temperature

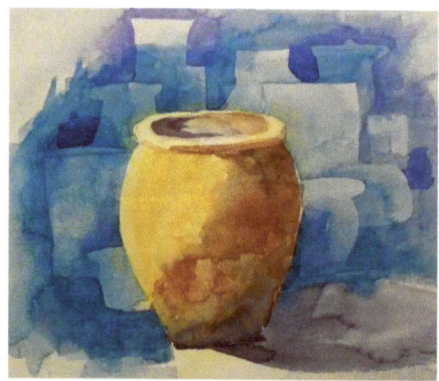

Each primary color, Red, Yellow, and Blue, has a

warm and a cool color.

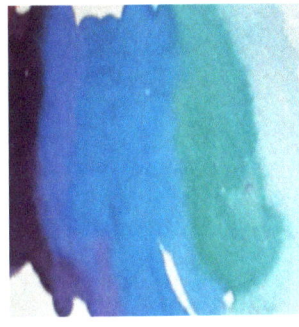

What's Cool Color?
Cool Colors
Purple, Blue, Green,

We know that snow is icy and cold. The cool colors have a cold feeling. The colors in a morning sunrise are cool colors, Purple, Blue, and Green.

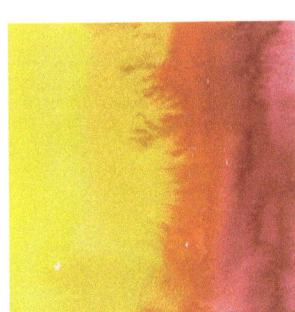

What's Warm Color?
Warm Colors
Yellow, Orange, Red

Think of a warm summer sunset, Hot Red peppers, ripe banana, all warm color Yellows, Orange and Red.

In the palette wells, place a warm color next to a cool color for each primary color. See the example below on warm and cool colors.

PRIMARY COLOR TEMPERATURE
Color has temperature!

Cool	Warm
Lemon Yellow	New Gamboge Yellow

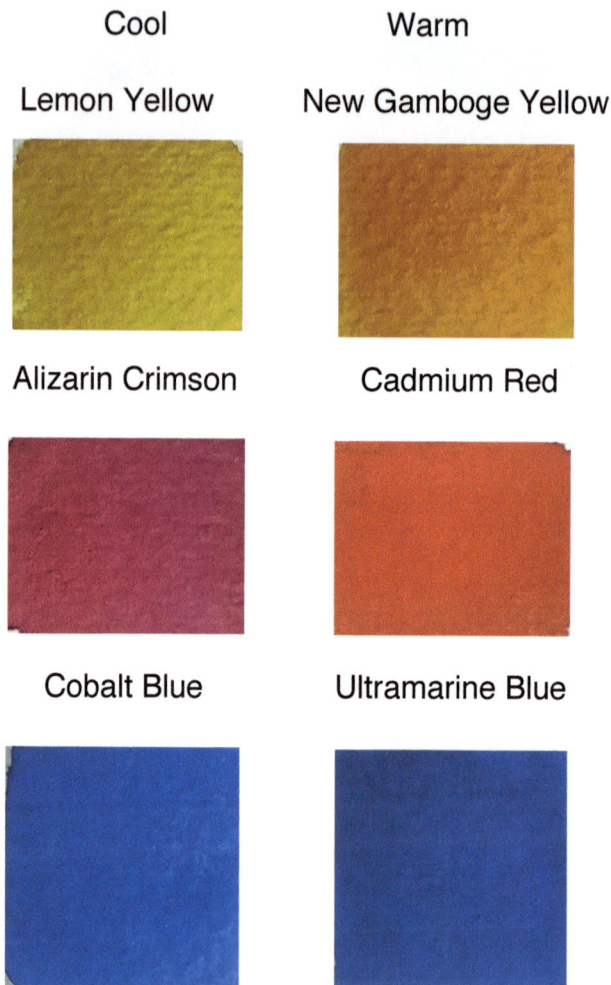

Alizarin Crimson   Cadmium Red

Cobalt Blue   Ultramarine Blue

An essential point you need to remember, do not mix the warm temperature colors with the cool temperature colors, causing the colors to look muddy. I know I mentioned this already, but I thought it important enough to mention again.

TIP:
Playing with color on paper by stroking it over and over again will dull the color and overwork the paper.

How to paint on Paper
Place a stroke, lift the brush, reload, and place another stroke alongside just touching the edge of the first stroke. Keep the freshness, luminosity, and clarity of color alive on the paper. No mud. No dull color.

Placing Warm and Cool color temperatures next to each other will work, but do not mix color temperatures. Use this warm next to cool color technique at the paintings center of interest. The warm and cool color will set up a visual zing, or a sense of visual vibration when placing warm and cool colors next to each other. How exciting!

Painting On Location

Painting in the Park
Painting on location is a visual gift for the artist. Every artist would benefit from going outside to SEE shape, object placement, shadows, time of day, and color intensity. I take one day a month to go out in the elements of the day, looking for contrast, and what visual story I'd like to paint.

Early one morning I loaded the car with painting gear and drove to Hesperia Lakes in my hometown. I parked near the lake and walked up the embankment. Looking out over this small lake, I saw reflections, ducks, geese, flora, and fauna. I opened my easel, set up my painting gear, and started to sketch. I was listening to the birds, sketching shapes, and could hear the honking of geese in the distance.

It did not take long to get a sketch on paper, and I was ready to paint. I could hear the geese honking, and I was aware they were on the move. I finished my first watercolor wash in light values and looked up over my easel to see about 50 geese walking directly towards me. I stopped painting and breathing. I couldn't outrun them, so I stayed put, kept painting, and started to talk to myself.

The geese walked as if they had control, and I believed they did. Waddling up to me, they honked continually. Once they surrounded me, all sat down and started peening their feathers. I looked around and saw nearly fifty geese sitting all around me. Panic was my first thought! Then, I calmed down and realized I didn't feel threatened but felt protected.

I continued to paint while the geese sat calmly around me. I could see a couple casually talking as they walked towards me. The geese stood up, honking loudly, as if telling the strangers to leave. The couple realized what was going on and changed direction. The geese quieted and sat back down. Knowing all was under their control, I felt the fold of protection as their treasured prisoner.

Once again the geese were unsettled, I looked around and spotted the ranger walking in my direction with food for the geese. FOOD! The geese got up and started to run towards the food. The honking and mass migration got the children in the park so excited they ran with the geese.

Notes and Ideas

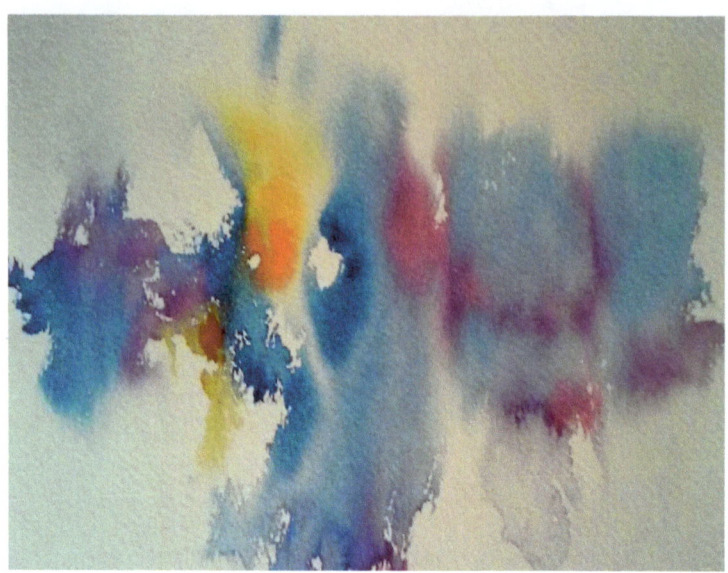

4

Color Schemes

Use A Color Wheel To Create Color Schemes

Select a Color Scheme before you put color to paper. Use your color wheel to do this selection process.

Review the six examples of Color Schemes below. I have described each one to help you get the idea of how to use a Color Scheme.

Ask yourself

Using what color scheme will tell your visual story?
Using what color scheme will show the mood of the day?
Using what color scheme will indicate the time of day?

Each Color Scheme has its quality and excitement. Delve into these examples so you can make a right choice before you start to paint your visual story.

Take the time to paint these examples, and keep them close to your easel to remind you of color scheme choices. Knowing what color scheme to use eliminates the temptation to use all eighteen to twenty colors in your palette.

Monochromatic

Analogous

Analogous with Complement

Complement

Split Complement

Triadic

Monochromatic Color
Using one color, change the value by adding water.

This Blue color has many values and can be used to paint a complete painting.

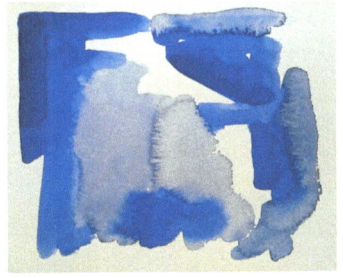

Light~Medium~Dark
Tone~Neutral~Intense

Analogous Color
The trick to Harmonious Color is to work with

Analogous Color Scheme.

Analogous means colors
next to each other on
the Color Wheel, Green,
Blue, and Purple. These
colors mix in a pleasing
way when mixing any
two of the three colors.

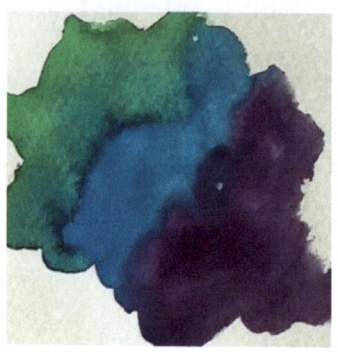

These Analogous colors when mixed in equal
amounts will create black.

Analogous with Complement Color

Analogous color uses any combination of three colors
next to each other on the color wheel. Add the color
directly across from the analogous color choice to
select its complement color.

Applying a complement color to analogous color will
gray or darken that color, building the darks

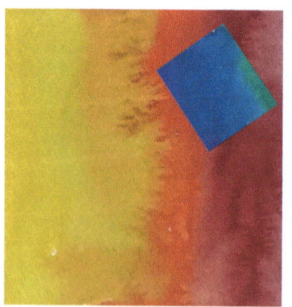

necessary to tell your visual
story.

See what happens using the
complement color Blue. The
eye travels directly to the
complement color area.

Use a small amount of blue to mingle with one
Analogous color, graying that color. Add water to
lighten value.

Complement Color

To make a unified painting in harmonious colors, use the primary color and its complement color.
SEE the examples below.

Equally, mix a primary color and its complement to make a neutral gray color.

Using this formula for a Color Scheme will give your painting unity. Remember you can change its value by adding water.

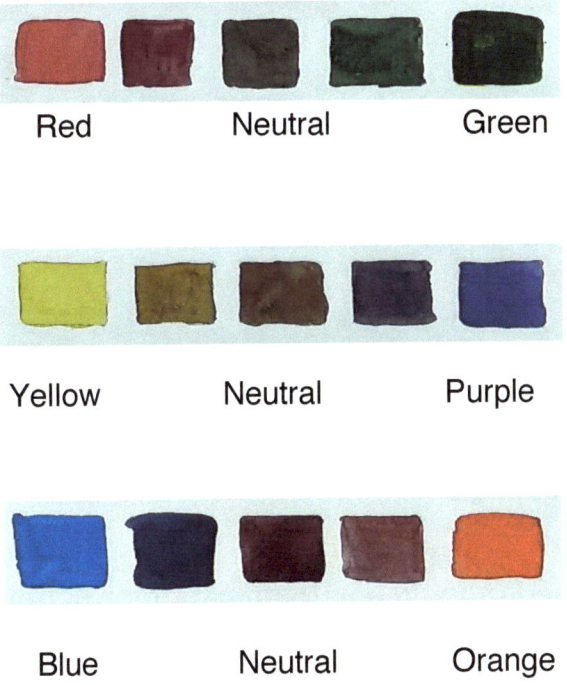

Red   Neutral   Green

Yellow   Neutral   Purple

Blue   Neutral   Orange

Split Complementary Color
Select a primary color. Directly across the color wheel, find its complement. Then use the color on the right and left of that complementary color.

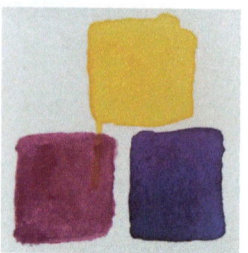

Triadic Color
Think of a triangle. Place the triangle on the color wheel. Align one point at the dominant color, and the triangle will point to the other Triadic Colors.

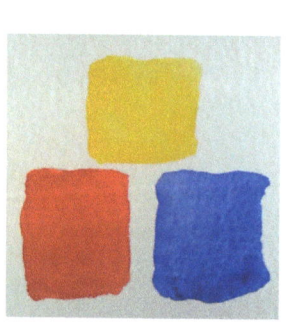
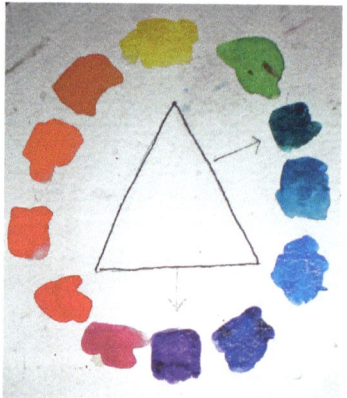

Value Change

Unity, Harmony, and Dynamic Color Scheme
* Add Water to tone or lighten color
* Add a complement color to gray or darken color

Decide on a Color Scheme before you start your painting, assuring harmony in your painting.

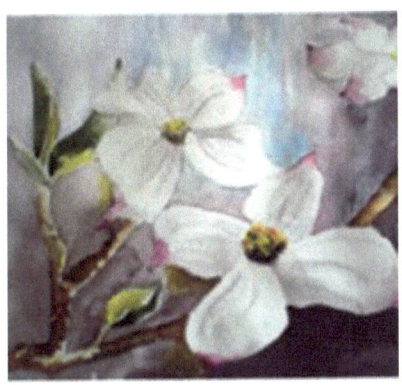

Analogous Color Scheme   **Compliment**
Green   Magenta
Cerulean
Purple

Working with the dominant cool color side of the color wheel, using touches of warm color adds visual excitement!

The cerulean is the eye candy that sets the background apart. It sets up depth, with a sense of cool colors that varies in value.

The warm dark purple foreground shows off hard edges and sharp contrast. What an attention grabber!

The dark center of the flower is in the center of interest area. The sharp contract of the white pedal and dark flower center directs the viewer's eye.

Dominate Color Schemes

High Key
Light and Airy
Light Values

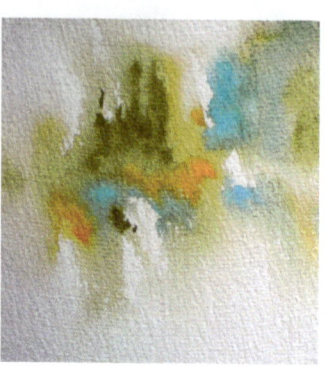

Using High Key colors will
create the atmosphere of
your painting. High Key will
be a fair weather painting
with bright colors and a
happy scene.

Low Key
Dark and Quiet
Dark Values

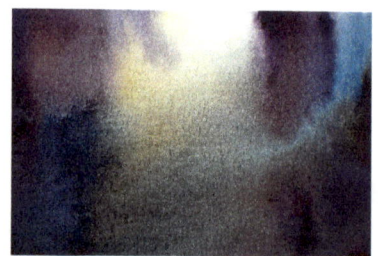

Using Low Key colors
will create the
atmosphere of your painting. Low Key will be a rough
weather painting with darker colors and shadowy
scene.
Mysterious!

Notes and Ideas

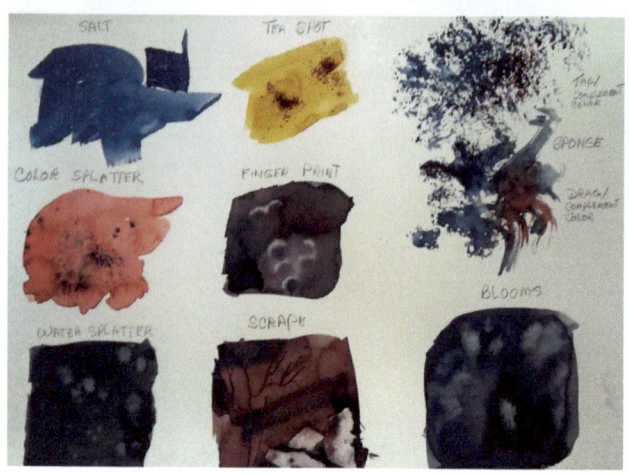

5

Color and Texture

Create the look of texture by disturbing the wet surface of the watercolor paper. Using these techniques will help tell your visual story.

Salt

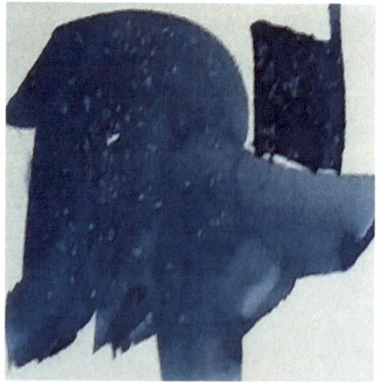

Salt crystals can be bought in different sizes, large, medium, and small. These sizes will determine how much color will lift. Salt crystals placed on damp paper will absorb the color leaving the white paper. Darker value color when sprinkled with salt will absorb the dark watercolor, and the white paper will show through. Dark against light values are attractive. When dry the crystals will brush off the watercolor paper.

Salt Instruction: Working with a darker color, put down a stroke, before the wet color dries, sprinkle SALT. Sprinkle sparingly too much salt in one area the crystals will stick together and hard or impossible to brush off the paper when dry.

TEA

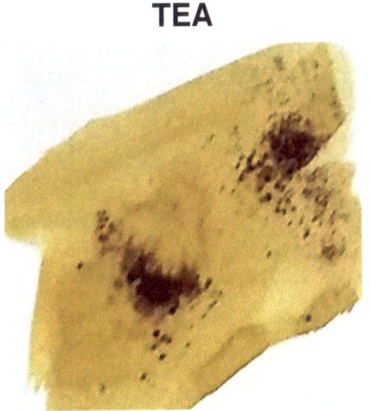

Instant Tea will dissolve on wet paper that has lost its glisten. Tea will transfer its brown color leaving spontaneous spots and large brown areas around the wet paper. The damp or wet paper will dissolve the tea and leave a brown spot. A banana has these markings, a good reference.

Sea Sponge

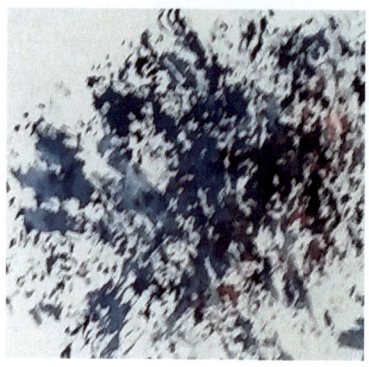

Tap a wet Sea Sponge loaded with color onto damp watercolor paper to show shapes. Stamping can be with multiple colors; this will add depth and variety, a good way to fill in tree leaves and bushes.

Splatter

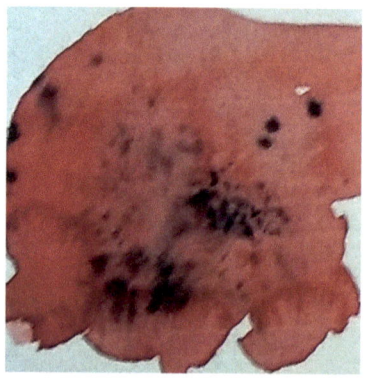

Splatter happens when a brush loaded with color is hit or jarred forcing the color to fall from the brush. Spontaneous splatter on dry paper or damp paper creates a textured look. Use complement colors like Orange with Blue splatter to set up a visual zing.

Finger Print

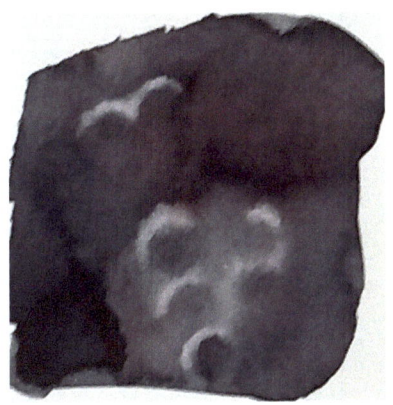

Finger Print on damp color will leave impressions of circles. These finger print circles give the illusion of a field of flowers simply by adding a stems and leaves.

Sponge Drag With Complement Color

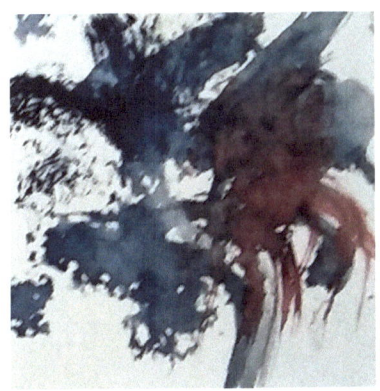

The sponge is a useful texture tool. Pick up one color or two colors and sponge on with a light swipe or use a heavy placement of the sponge on paper causing a larger color area. If you're satisfied, leave to dry. If you want to add more energy, wet your brush and move some of the colors around, pushing the dots together and mingling the colors will look spontaneous and eye catching.

Water Splatter

Water Splatter has unusual patterns and sizes.

Method 1: I flick water off my fingertips around the interest area.

Method 2: I load a brush and then hit the handle with another brush to jar the water drops off and onto the paper.

Remember splatter works well on damp paper.

How to tell when the paper is damp? The wet paint glistens. When the paint starts to dry, the shine disappears, and it is time to splatter the water onto the paper. The water drop patterns are irregular and interesting, better than touching a brush to damp paper and trying to make a natural pattern.

Crease and Scrape

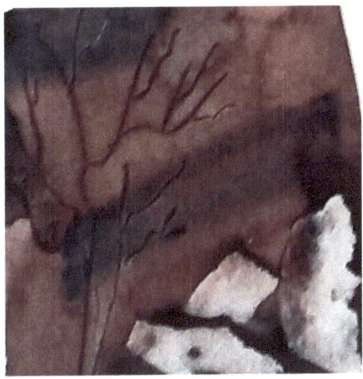

Use a sharp object, like a palette knife or the bevel on a brush handle, to indent in the paper. Place a brush stroke across the paper indent. The watercolor will flow into and fill the dent, making that area darker and showing the crease design. This technique works well with brush, weeds, and stems.

The next scraping technique is using the side of a palette knife or credit card edge to scrape an area clear of paint. This method is excellent for creating boulders and flag stone pathways to change values on an object.

Blooms and Blossoms

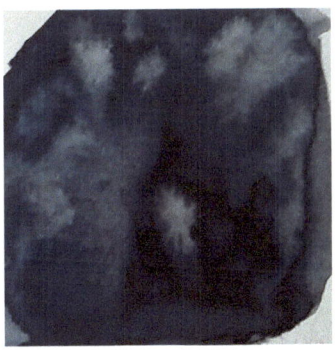

Play with edges, load a large brush with water, bring over the area, and drop or slightly touch the wet paper. Let the intrusive water work magic while the paper lays flat on the table. Do not touch again with a brush, or the first water drops will change. Let dry to see what interesting shapes develop. Discharged color will react differently, depending on the amount of water on the paper and the amount of water on the brush.

Mingling

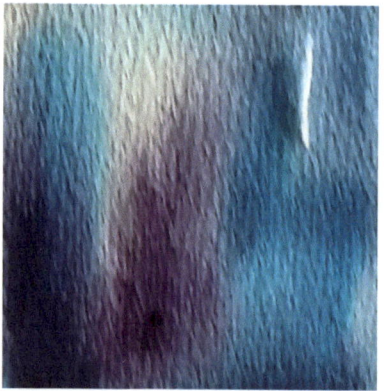

A fun way to play with edges load a brush with water, bring over the area, and drop or slightly touch the wet paper. Let the intrusive water work magic while the paper lays flat on the table. Do not contact with a brush, or the first water drips will alter. Let dry to see what new shapes appear. Discharged color will react differently, depending on the amount of water on the paper and the amount of water on the brush.

Merging

Merging color is a technique handled with a brush. Paint one color on paper. Add another color, just touching the edge of the first color, showing an attractive blurred edge and gray color. Using colors that are different temperature will add a zing or color vibration to your composition. Do not mix color, but lay one color alongside a dried color for that color zing.

Notes and Ideas

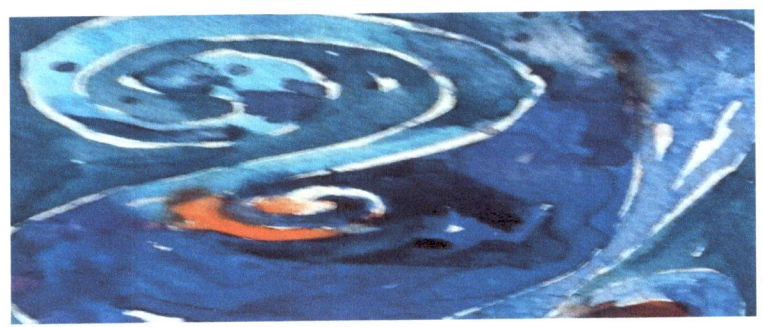

Word Clarity

Analogous ~ Use any combination of three colors next to each other on the color wheel.

Add two colors together to change the color.

Add more water to change the value.

Page 41

Analogous with Complement ~ Use any combination of three colors next to each other on the color wheel. Then look directly across the color wheel to find the complement color.

Page 42

Background

Divide the watercolor paper into unequal horizontal thirds. The top section of paper shows background area. Use cool color temperature for the illusion of distance.

Page 13

Color Theory

Color Theory is a vast subject. I have touched on the

beginning pointers of Color Theory in this book.
Read, understand, and practice so that you will build a
solid foundation of knowledge about Color Theory.

Page 40

Complementary Color ~ Choose a primary color on
the Color Wheel and look directly across the main
color to find its complementary color.

Add the primary color to its complement, and that will
gray the complement color. Equal amounts of the
primary color and complement color will create true
gray a middle-value color.

Add more water to change the value.

Page 43

Dark Values ~ Mix three Primary Colors using more
of one primary color, will give a dark blackish color
with a hint of the dominant primary color.

Page 28

Foreground
Divide the watercolor paper into unequal horizontal
thirds. The bottom of the paper is foreground area.
Foreground has the look of warm, intense color with
some edges that lead the eye into the painting.

Page 13

Grayed Color ~ Mixing unequal parts of a Primary
Color with its Complement color.

Page 22

Hue ~ A word meaning, Color
Page 27

Luminosity ~ A layer of dried transparent color will show the white glow of watercolor paper through the color.
Page 22

Middle Ground

Divide the watercolor paper into unequal horizontal thirds. The middle of paper is the middle ground area.

Middle Ground has the look of neutral color with lost and found edges.
Page 13

Mixing Grayed Colors

Using complement colors will make grayed colors. The amount of a complement color will influence the value of grayed color. Red with a touch of Green will make a light grayed Red. Green with a slight touch of Red will make a light grayed Green. Equal amounts of complement colors will make a true neutral gray color.
Page 27

Monochromatic ~ One color, intense out of the tube, add water to change from Intense to tone color.

Use three values to make a form, Light, Medium, and Dark, creating a beautiful painting from one Monochromatic color.

Add Complement Color to any one of the Analogous Colors to gray its color. That adds another color. Add more water to change the value of color.

Page 41

Overworked ~ Lifting color by aggressively scrubbing an area destroying the paper texture. BIG problem!

Stroking the color again and again in the same wet spot will over wet the paper causing the sizing to fail and the paper to deteriorate. With sizing gone, this paper will no longer accept color in the same way. Paper will react like a blotter.

Page 26

Reference Charts
I challenge you to create reference charts.
Value Scale
Color Wheel
Color Intensity to Tone
Warm/Cool Color Temperature
Analogous Color Scheme choices

Place all the Analogous Color Scheme options close to you when designing a painting helping you choose the right color combinations to tell your visual story.

Temperature Warm/Cool ~ Place a warm color next to a cool color, and this will set up a visual vibration. Do not mix Warm and Cool temperatures as this will create MUD, a dull, flat, uninteresting color.

Page 36

Triadic ~ Three Colors evenly spaced around the color wheel, like a triangle shape.

Add one Triadic color to another to change color.

Add water to change the value.

Page 44

* * *

Working with color is a large subject. I touched on the beginning points of color theory in this book.

Notes and Ideas

Artist/Teacher/Author

Barbara's Update

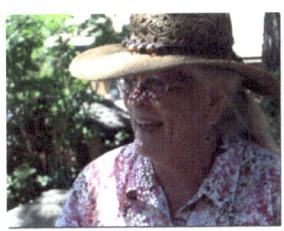

This year I decided to stay in town and paint at my home-based studio. My focus is to experiment with color schemes and textures.

I have a backyard Cabernet Sauvignon vineyard to manage. This vineyard has inspired many of my paintings. Yes, I make wine. I harvest the vineyard and start the wine making process in late August or the first part of September.

I am working on my third book in the Watercolor Action Series.

"Watercolor ~ Artistic Perspective"
Working thru the challenges of designing the page with object placement, size, values, and line.

Check my website www.barbaraparish.weebly.com for updates on exhibits, books, book signings, watercolor workshops, and watercolor demonstrations.

Let me know how you are doing on your painting adventures. barbaraparish@verizon.net

Barbara

Books

2016 Watercolor ~ Meet The Brushes
Create the Stroke and Control the Flow

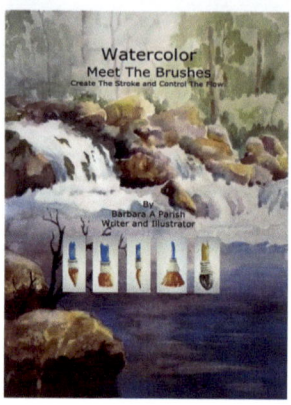

2017 Watercolor ~ Value to Color Parallel
See the Value and Match the Color

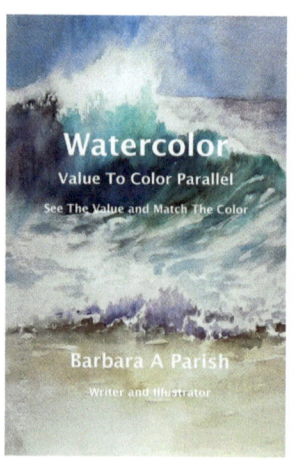

* Coming in December 2017
Watercolor ~ Artistic Perspective
Linear and Aerial